Unshakable

HOPE

DESTINY IMAGE BOOKS BY DEREK PRINCE

Longing for His Appearing

Why Bad Things Happen to God's People

Unshakable
HOPE

JOYFUL EXPECTATION IN EVERY SEASON

DEREK PRINCE

DESTINY IMAGE® PUBLISHERS, INC.

P.O. Box 310, Shippensburg, PA 17257-0310

"Promoting Inspired Lives."

This book and all other Destiny Image and Destiny Image Fiction books are available at Christian bookstores and distributors worldwide.

Cover design by Eileen Rockwell

Interior design by Terry Clifton

For more information on foreign distributors, call 717-532-3040.

Reach us on the Internet: www.destinyimage.com.

ISBN 13 TP: 978-0-7684-4845-0

ISBN 13 eBook: 978-0-7684-4846-7

ISBN 13 HC: 978-0-7684-4848-1

ISBN 13 LP: 978-0-7684-4847-4

For Worldwide Distribution, Printed in the U.S.A.

1 2 3 4 5 6 7 8 / 23 22 21 20 19

CONTENTS

FOREWORD

ARE YOU LOOKING FOR REAL HOPE? IN THE BOOK YOU are about to read, Derek Prince makes this statement:

> *If it is real hope, based on the substance of real faith, it will affect the way we live.*

Can you think of one person who is not searching for that kind of hope? A hope so genuine it makes life different and better? Would you place yourself in that category?

You may find it interesting that Derek Prince put himself in that category. Even after he became a believer in Jesus Christ—even through his early days as a Christian pastor—Derek faced regular battles with hopelessness. It was his own desperate quest for hope, and the help he subsequently found in God's Word, that motivated him to share so frequently on this topic. His solid teaching is based on his own deep, personal experience. This is the core of the book you are about to read.

Here is some very good news for you, dear reader. If you are on a search for genuine hope—the kind that will affect your entire outlook on life—it is available to you. In fact, by picking up this book, you have taken the first step on the path to finding real hope.

Romans 5:5 says, *"Now hope does not disappoint"* (NKJV). It is our sincere prayer that you will be able to say the same about the book you are about to read— *Unshakable Hope.*

The International Publishing Team
of Derek Prince Ministries

Chapter 1

THREE POWERFUL REALITIES

PERHAPS YOU ARE FAMILIAR WITH THE SAYING: *"WHERE there is life, there is hope."* There is a good deal of truth in that maxim. But the opposite is also true: *"Where there is hope, there is life."* In my opinion, hopelessness is one of the saddest conditions in human experience. I can hardly think of anything sadder than to be hopeless. Yet uncounted millions in our world today are hopeless people. But thanks be to God, we do not need to be hopeless!

There is a hope which can liberate you and me from the constraints of this world, with all its petty concerns and worries. It can liberate you from your own inadequacies, your own inabilities, your own weaknesses, and your own frustrations. You and I do not have to be shut up in the prison of this world. What can liberate us? Hope.

I believe that *genuine hope,* as presented in the Scriptures, can give you and me a completely new outlook on life. That is why the theme I have chosen for this study is "Hope." I trust that what we discover together in these pages will help you grasp what hope is, how important it is, and most of all, how you may have it.

Let me define hope as it is used in the Bible: *Hope is a serene, confident expectation of good.* Would you like to have that kind of hope for your life and future? I trust by the end of this study you will have come closer to the reality of this kind of hope.

ETERNAL FOUNDATIONS

By way of introduction to the theme of hope, let's look at First Corinthians, chapter 13, verse 13, where Paul says:

> *And now abide faith, hope, love, these three; but the greatest of these is love* (NKJV).

In that verse, Paul presents us with the three great abiding spiritual realities of the Christian faith. Much of what we experience in life may come and go. Some of it may be important or significant for a certain period of time or for certain situations we might face. But there are three realities that abide forever: *faith, hope, and love.*

Most Christians have heard much preaching about faith and a good deal about love. However, most of us have heard comparatively little about hope.

That was my condition many years ago when I was in desperate need of help from God. I had heard a lot of messages on faith. I had heard some preaching on love. But the message I needed in that particular situation was *hope.* To meet that need in me, the Holy Spirit had to take me directly to the Scripture, because there were no sermons that I knew of on the subject of hope. It was through the Word of God that the Holy Spirit met my need.

As a result of my own deep need for hope, and my experience of searching for it, I have a particular concern that people understand the importance of hope. As I said, I trust that what we share on this topic in this study will help you to grasp what hope is, how important it is, and how you may have it.

HOPE IS ESSENTIAL

We spoke of the three abiding realities: faith, hope, and love. Here is an important point. Hope is the reality that is necessary to maintain both faith and love. In due course, I will show you in various ways that unless we have hope, our faith will leak out, and our love will fail. So, hope is not an option; it is a component that is essential to the fullness of the Christian life.

What exactly did "the fullness of the Christian life" look like in the early church? In First Thessalonians 1:2–4, Paul presents a picture of God's people, the Christians of Thessalonica, enjoying their full inheritance. They have faith, they have hope, and they have love. Please notice that he mentions all three of these virtues as he gives thanks to God for them. Here is what Paul says:

> *We give thanks to God always for all of you, making mention of you in our prayers* [Why does he give thanks?]; *constantly bearing in mind your work of faith and labor of love and steadfastness of hope in our Lord Jesus Christ in the presence of our God and Father, knowing, brethren beloved by God, His choice of you* (NAS 1977).

It is clear that the spiritual condition of those Christians in Thessalonica convinced Paul they were really people chosen by God. What he saw in them were those three abiding realities: faith, love, and hope. In his praise for the Thessalonians, Paul uses a characteristic word to describe what is special about each of those realities. He speaks about the *work* of faith, the *labor* of love, and the *steadfastness* of hope.

VITAL ATTRIBUTES

In the sections that follow, we will focus on each of those phrases for a moment and meditate on them. First of all, faith must be expressed by works or by actions. Faith that doesn't act is dead faith. Here is what Paul says in that regard in Galatians 5:6:

> *For in Christ Jesus neither circumcision nor uncircumcision means anything, but faith working through love.*

Please notice, it is faith *working* through love. The book of James says the same thing in another way. In James 2:26 we read, *"For just as the body without the spirit is dead, so also faith without works is dead."*

We see that the characteristic expression of faith is works. This means action—doing something that is the outcome of our faith and expresses our faith. Faith without works is a dead faith.

In the passage we quoted at the beginning of this section, in Paul's word to the Thessalonians, he also speaks about their "labor of love." The word "labor" means really hard work. Isn't that so characteristic of true love? True love does not just sit around and sympathize. True love gets in where the action is, rolls up its sleeves, and does something tangible. Love involves a cost of labor. It demands an expenditure—possibly one involving weariness and sleeplessness. Love labors. It is not just a passive emotion. Love is an active, driving force that moves people to sacrificial labor on behalf of others.

In the same passage cited earlier, we then come to Paul's phrase about hope. Paul commends these disciples in Thessalonica on *"the steadfastness of [your] hope."* He was implying that hope is connected to steadfastness, endurance, perseverance. Without those qualities of steadfastness, endurance, and perseverance that hope produces, we may easily lose the benefits of the first two virtues—that is, faith and love.

THE SOURCE OF HOPE

How, then, does hope come? How may we have this kind of hope which is so real and so necessary? The answer is that hope is the direct outcome of the new birth. It is the direct outcome of being born again by the Holy Spirit through faith in Jesus Christ. It is not through just general faith in Jesus Christ, but rather a specific faith in His death, burial, and resurrection. This truth is confirmed by what Peter says in First Peter, chapter 1, verse 3:

> *Praise be to the God and Father of our Lord Jesus Christ! In his great mercy he has given us new birth into a living hope through the resurrection of Jesus Christ from the dead* (NIV).

Please notice this very significant phrase: *"new birth into a living hope through the resurrection of Jesus Christ from the dead."* It tells us that when we believe in the death of Jesus Christ on our behalf and then in His resurrection from the dead by the power of God, we are born again; we have a new birth. We are born into a living hope. Not just some dead theology, but a living, vibrating hope.

Hope comes to us through the resurrection of Jesus Christ from the dead. We must clearly understand this ultimate historical basis for all hope. True hope is founded upon the resurrection of Jesus. Without the resurrection of Jesus, life would be hopeless. It is the resurrection of Jesus which brings us into a living hope.

HOPE CONTINUES

It is important for us to realize that this hope that we receive at the new birth must continue until the consummation of our salvation. We just looked at one quote from First Peter. But there is another vital truth in that epistle, which occurs just a little further on in the same first chapter:

> *Therefore, prepare your minds for action, keep sober in spirit, fix your hope completely on the grace to be brought to you at the revelation of Jesus Christ* (1 Peter 1:13).

What Peter is saying in this verse is that the process of salvation is not yet complete. It is ultimately going to be consummated by the revelation of Jesus Christ. In the meanwhile, you and I have to fix our hope completely on that future event. In other words, the ultimate focus of all Christian hope is the second coming of the Lord Jesus

Christ. As we make our way through this life, we need to obey that injunction of Peter. We must fix our hope completely on the grace and blessing that will be ours through the return of Jesus in glory.

Until the End

Similar to this important principle, the writer of Hebrews brings out another very important facet of hope in Hebrews 3:6:

> *But Christ was faithful as a Son over His house—whose house we are, if we hold fast our confidence and the boast of our hope firm until the end.*

Once again, please notice that this hope must be maintained throughout the entirety of our lives. You and I cannot give up hoping. We must hold on firmly and intentionally until our hope is fulfilled by the event for which we hope. The writer of Hebrews makes this clear in the admonition above; in order to be a part of the people of God, we must *"hold fast our confidence and the boast of our hope firm until the end."*

The kind of hope we must maintain is not just a passive, inner expectation. Rather, it is a conviction in our hearts that is very strong, and very confident. It is a hope that boasts—not in itself, of course—but in the Lord.

This instruction for us to boast, to maintain a verbal expression of our hope, is part of what God has provided for us. Boasting goes along with hope, and hope, in turn, goes along with faith and love. We have to maintain this confident boasting of our hope—this continual assertion of our expectation of the coming of the Lord Jesus—until the end of our lives or until Jesus comes in glory.

ASKING FOR HOPE

Let me close this first chapter by asking you a question. Do you have the kind of hope we have been talking about here? Can you honestly say you have the vibrant hope described in the verses we have covered in this chapter? Perhaps you would have to admit that you are in a similar condition to where I was before the Holy Spirit opened my eyes.

If you know that you have a deep need for hope to arise in your heart, that is a good recognition—and a good reason to keep reading. Before you read another page, let's ask the Lord together to help us discover and receive the hope we so desperately need.

> *Lord, I'm not sure that I have a living hope to the degree I need at this time. I know, from what I have seen so far, that hope can be a powerful force in my life. I want that hope, Lord. Please begin the process today of bringing true hope to life in my heart. Thank You, Lord. Amen.*

Chapter 2

RELATIONSHIP BETWEEN FAITH AND HOPE

IN OUR FIRST CHAPTER, I POINTED OUT THAT IN THE Christian life there are three abiding realities, three truths that always remain: faith, hope, and love. I also pointed out certain characteristics of each of these virtues. *Faith* should produce work, or action, because without action it is a dead faith. *Love* produces labor—hard, sacrificial, self-giving work on behalf of others. Love does not just use polite religious clichés; love rolls up its sleeves and gets to work where the work is hardest. And when we think of *hope's* main characteristics, these three words come to light: steadfastness, endurance, and perseverance.

So those are the characteristics of the three, abiding realities. Faith produces action; love produces labor; and hope produces steadfastness, endurance, and perseverance. We saw clearly that if we don't have the perseverance hope supplies, we are very liable to lose the benefits of the other two—faith and love.

THE NATURE OF HOPE

In the previous chapter, we also considered two additional truths concerning hope. First, we addressed this question: How does hope come to us? Peter gives us the answer in First Peter 1:3:

> *Praise be to the God and Father of our Lord Jesus Christ! In his great mercy he has given us new birth into a living hope through the resurrection of Jesus Christ from the dead* (NIV).

Hope is the direct outcome of being born again through faith in Jesus Christ. The new birth brings us *into a living hope.* We are not born again into some dead theology or theory, but into a living, vibrating anticipation based on the resurrection of Jesus Christ. When Jesus rose from the dead, it was the ultimate victory of hope over hopelessness!

Second, we learned that hope must have a target—it must be focused on something. We read this in First Peter 1:13.

> *Therefore, gird your minds for action, keep sober in spirit, fix your hope completely on the grace to be brought to you at the revelation of Jesus Christ* (NAS 1977).

We are all in a process—the process of salvation. But it is not yet complete. It will be consummated by the revelation of Jesus Christ. In the meanwhile, our mandate is to fix our hope steadfastly on His second coming.

These two truths are essential to us. Hope is living and vibrant—and the focus of our hope must be the revelation or appearing of our Lord Jesus Christ.

FAITH AND HOPE

In this chapter we are going to explore the relationship between faith and hope. Through the year, as I have ministered to many thousands of Christians, I have seen a consistent tendency emerge. I have discovered from my own experience that many believers confuse faith with hope and hope with faith.

To introduce this segment on the relationship between faith and hope, let me begin by pointing out an important distinction: faith is in the *present*, hope is in the *future*. If you have a faith which is only in the future, you really don't have faith. What you have is hope.

For example, when people would ask me to pray for them, my first question would be, "Do you believe God can do this?"

Many times, they would answer, "I hope He will."

As good as that reply may be, hoping is not the same as having faith. They were simply hoping God would do what they were asking of Him. However, we must understand that the results promised to faith do not flow from hope. Each is important, but neither is a substitute for the other.

Faith is in the heart, while hope is in the mind. Faith is in the now, while hope is in the future. Both are legitimate, but we must have them in the right place and in the right relationship.

THE SUBSTANCE OF FAITH

Let's look at the biblical definition of faith (which, by the way, also includes the word *hope*) in Hebrews 11, verses 1–3:

> *Now faith is the assurance* [Greek, "substance"] *of things hoped for, the conviction of things not seen. For by it the men of old* [that is, the Old Testament saints] *gained approval. By faith we understand that the worlds were prepared by the word of God, so that what is seen was not made out of things which are visible.*

These verses contain several very important statements. First, we notice that faith is a *substance*. It is not just a theory; it is not just a theology; it is not just a doctrine. You can have all those without having faith. Truly, faith has to be a "substance" for us.

The Greek word for "substance" means "the underlying basis" or "foundation" of something. Faith is the underlying bedrock of assurance on which hope is supported. To have hope without faith may be self-deception, but when you have faith, then you are entitled to hope. *Faith is the substance of things hoped for.*

Therefore, in order for hope to be real, it must be built on faith. But then the verse says that faith is based on "things not seen"—on that which is not visible. Faith is ultimately based on the Word of God, and lays hold of the fact that the whole universe was brought into being by the invisible Word of God. In other words, what we see around us was created out of that which cannot be seen. Our faith is based upon the unseen, eternal reality of God's Word. Hope, in turn, is based on faith.

As I said already (but it warrants saying it again because it is so important)—faith is here and now. Faith is a substance, something which we really have right now. But hope, based on that faith, looks to the future.

It is important not to confuse the two, because God has promised results to faith which are not promised to hope. It is also very important to realize that hope is only valid when it is based on faith. Faith, in turn, is based on God's Word. So the ultimate basis of both faith and hope is the Word of God.

HOPE DEFINED

A lot of people think they have hope. They may justifiably use that word, but their use of the term "hope" is not actually in line with the scriptural meaning of the word. You and I are only entitled to say we have hope when our hope is based on the real and present substance of faith. Then we are talking about having hope along scriptural lines.

Any other kind of hope is mere wishful thinking. It is possible that such a hope may be fulfilled, but there is no guarantee. The only hope which is guaranteed its fulfillment is a hope based on genuine faith.

So again, bear in mind that faith is in the present. Faith is a substance. Faith is here and now. Faith is based on the unseen reality of the Word of God. Hope, in turn, is based on that faith. The kind of hope which is based on genuine faith is guaranteed fulfillment. However, any other kind of hope is no better than wishful thinking.

Let me mention again my personal definition of hope. This is how I understand hope as it is presented in the Bible: *Hope is a serene, confident expectation of good.* Hope is both serene (peaceful) and confident (firm).

LOOKING FOR HOPE

There is an aspect of hope which I have already mentioned. However, because it is so important, I would like to examine it more closely. Let me summarize that aspect of hope: *The ultimate focus of all true hope is the return of Jesus Christ in glory.*

Paul affirms this truth in Titus 2:11–13:

> *For the grace of God has appeared, bringing salvation to all men, instructing us to deny ungodliness and worldly desires and to live sensibly, righteously and godly in the present age, looking for the blessed hope and the appearing of the glory of our great God and Savior, Christ Jesus.*

The last verse, verse 13, is what you might call "the punch line" for the rest of the passage—the explanation of all that goes before. What does it say? *"Looking for the blessed hope and the appearing of the glory of our great God and Savior, Jesus Christ."* We are to look for that ultimate hope of all Christians which stretches beyond time and out into eternity. What is that blessed hope? It is the appearing of the glory of our great God and Savior, Christ Jesus. (Significantly, Paul calls Jesus "our great God.")

How does "looking for the blessed hope of Jesus' appearing" affect our lives? To answer that question, let's return to Paul's beginning words in verse 11: *"For the grace of God has appeared, bringing salvation to all men, instructing us."*

Please notice that grace instructs us. Grace has the capacity in our lives to teach us. What does it instruct us to do? "*To deny ungodliness and worldly desires and to live sensibly, righteously and godly in the present age.*" Why do we live that way? Because we are looking forward to a new age which will be brought about by the return of the Lord Jesus Christ. We want to be ready when He comes, and we don't want to be ashamed to be in His presence.

So, the hope of Jesus' appearing motivates us to godly living. It is the greatest single motivator in the New Testament. In his first epistle, the apostle John wrote, "*everyone who has this hope in Him purifies himself, just as He* [Jesus Christ] *is pure*" (1 John 3:3 NKJV). This kind of hope leads to self-purifying. If it is real hope, based on the substance of real faith, it will affect the way we live. Godly living is the first effect of our hope for the appearing of Jesus Christ in glory.

TIME AND ETERNITY

The second effect is related to the first one: having this hope releases us from the bondage of time. We are no longer slaves of just a few years of life. We are looking forward to eternity.

Because of the hope of Jesus' return, we are not overwhelmed by the disasters and the troubles of living in our times as other people seem to be. Why are they so anxious? Because they have nowhere else to look except at the world around them. They are constrained; they are shut up in just the few years that God gives them in this life.

In contrast, for us who have this glorious hope, our few years in this life are just a period of preparation for eternity. Because we have hope in the revelation of Jesus Christ, it inevitably affects the way we live. In fact, when we look at people who say they have this hope, we should see this same evidence and confidence in the way they live.

HOPE FOR YOU

Is this issue of godly living based on hope a new thought for you? If someone were to ask you if you have this kind of hope, what would you say? Even more, does your life say yes or no? Do you feel constrained by time, or are you looking beyond time to eternity?

Your heart may be telling you right now that you want to move forward into this kind of blessed hope. You long for the joy and freedom it can bring. If that is *truly* your desire, let's conclude this chapter with the following prayer for help from the Lord.

> *Lord, I want the kind of hope I have just read about. I am asking for Your help to receive this genuine hope. I want to be motivated to focus on You, pursue a godly life, have freedom from the bondage of time, and look forward to Your return.*
>
> *With faith in Your word, Lord, I ask You to let hope come to me—and I thank You in advance for answering my prayer. In Jesus' name. Amen.*

THE SOURCE
OF ALL HOPE

WE KNOW THAT IN OUR WORLD TODAY, MILLIONS OF people are suffering from hopelessness—including many sincere Christians. What can people do when they have lost all hope, or have no idea where to find hope? Fortunately, God has an answer to that important question. His answer will be the focus of this chapter.

Earlier, I shared from my own experience that there was a time in my life when I, too, had lost all hope. I found myself in desperate need of help from God. Thankfully, the Holy Spirit, our Helper and Comforter, directed my search to God's Word, and there He met my need. My own experience is the basis of my deep concern for Christians to understand and live in real, biblical hope—the kind that is revealed in the Scriptures. That is the purpose of this book.

If, at this moment, you are in the process of searching for renewed hope, please be encouraged. What God did for me, He can do for you! I fully believe that genuine hope can be rekindled in your heart. The theme we discuss in this chapter, *The Source of All Hope,* will help you in the process.

AN IMPORTANT RELATIONSHIP

Let's begin this chapter with a brief overview of some of the truths we have covered so far. It is important for us to keep in mind the close relationship between faith and hope. Faith is based on God's Word, which is invisible; hope is based on that faith. Faith is in the present—it is a substance which we have here and now. Hope, on the other hand, looks to the future. But the only *valid* kind of hope is that which is based on present faith. Any other kind of hope is mere wishful thinking. It may come true, but there is no guarantee.

We also learned that hope, although based on present faith, must be focused on something in the future. What should be the focus of our hope? The ultimate focus of all Christian hope is the return of Jesus Christ. This is *the blessed hope,* set before all true believers. We may have other hopes and dreams, but this is *the* hope.

Making Jesus' return our ultimate focus will have two main effects on the way we live. First of all, it will motivate us to live in a holy way. The expectation of Jesus' return was the single greatest motivator in the New Testament.

The second effect of this hope is that it will release us from the bondage of time. The people of this world don't have eternity in view—they are shut in a little prison of the few brief years God has allotted to them. And it is an uncertain prison, for no one knows how long they have to live. People with a mindset that focuses on this life have nothing to transcend it—and very little hope. But it is different for a believer in Jesus Christ. We also live in time, but our hope takes us beyond time into eternity. *Hope liberates us from the prison of time.*

THE SOURCE OF ALL HOPE

Earlier I offered my own personal definition of hope as I believe it is presented in the Bible: *Hope is a serene, confident expectation of good.* Hope is not just serene or passive; it is confident. Isn't that the kind of hope we all want and need? Here is the first truth we need to answer the question: How do we get this kind of confident hope? The source of all hope is the love of God. Paul affirms this truth in Second Thessalonians, chapter 2, verses 16 and 17.

> *Now may our Lord Jesus Christ Himself and God our Father, who has loved us and given us eternal comfort and good hope by grace, comfort and strengthen your hearts in every good work and word* (NAS 1977).

Aren't those beautiful, powerful words? As we meditate on the profundity of this verse, five important aspects emerge.

God's Love

The first truth we see is what we cited earlier: the source of hope is God's love. God loved us, and therefore He gave us *"eternal comfort and good hope by grace."* Always bear this in mind: The ultimate power behind the universe is the love of God. God is a Father, and when we know God as Father, we have this kind of hope—it is a gift of His love. It proceeds from a confidence in His unwavering love and faithfulness.

Through Christ

Second, although the source of hope is God's love, it comes to us *through Jesus Christ*. We know this because Paul mentions not only God our Father, but "our Lord Jesus Christ Himself." Jesus is the only channel through whom love from God and hope from God can come into our lives.

By Grace

The third feature of this hope is that it is a *gift*. But how do we receive it? *By grace*. Paul says God gave us *"eternal comfort and good hope by grace."* Please remember that grace cannot be earned. Anything that can be earned is *not* grace. The gifts and blessings that come by grace can only be received by faith. Therefore, you have to *receive* this hope—you simply cannot try to earn it. It does not come by trying to work out whether you are good enough. Nor does it come by trying to reason within yourself to find some rational basis why you ought to be hopeful.

Hope can only be received as a gift of God's love—given by His grace.

Beyond Time

Fourth, together with that phrase, "good hope," Paul says God has given us "eternal comfort." We have already stated this principle, but it bears repetition because it is so important: *With hope there comes a comfort that goes beyond time.* Our expectations, our anticipations, our satisfactions are not limited to this brief span of time. They possess an eternal quality. That word, "eternal," is such a rich word, such a vast word. It means "that which is not subject to time; that which is not in time; that which was before time and will be after time."

Eternal hope lifts us out of the confinement of this prison of time and puts us onto a different level—an eternal plane of living. We can walk this earth like kings, queens, and princes because we have this hope. We are no longer slaves of time; we have been liberated by the gift of hope—given to us through God's grace.

For Holiness

Finally, a point we have noted previously, but deserves repetition for emphasis—hope makes us strong for holy living. After Paul has spoken about the eternal comfort and the good hope, he says that God will *"comfort and strengthen your hearts in every good word and work."*

Let's be honest: hopeless people are weak people. They don't have any real motivation. When the going gets tough, they have nothing to make them hang in there. Their hands fall slack, they shrug their shoulders, and say, "Well, I suppose it's no use." But people who have this kind of eternal hope we are talking about have strength and resolve. In times of hardship and trouble, those people endure. They hold fast. God strengthens their hearts through eternal hope.

Let me just briefly recapitulate the five points we have noted from this passage in Thessalonians:

- The source for hope is God's love;

- It comes through Christ;

- It is a gift by grace;

- It is eternal;

- It makes us strong for holy living.

LIBERATED TO LIVE

As we conclude this chapter, I want to emphasize again the eternal nature of hope by looking at the word of Paul in Romans, chapter 14, verses 7-8.

> *For none of us lives for ourselves alone, and none of us dies for ourselves alone. If we live, we live for the Lord; and if we die, we die for the Lord. So, whether we live or die, we belong to the Lord* (NIV).

We do not live or die to ourselves alone. To be so self-focused is to be very lonely—and this world of ours is full of lonely people. They are shut up in prisons of their own selves. They live for themselves; they die by themselves. They have no other interests, and their concerns do not reach beyond themselves. They are in a prison of self.

But through Christ, we are liberated from this prison! Paul says we don't live to ourselves, nor do we die to ourselves. We live for Christ, and we die in Christ: *"Whether we live or whether we die, we belong to the Lord."* So, death has no real dominion over us. It has no terror for us. It is simply a release into a higher plane of living.

THE ULTIMATE ISSUES

It is so vital for us to understand that Christ has dealt with the ultimate issues we face—which are life and death. For people who subscribe to any kind of religion, faith, or philosophy which cannot deal with life and death issues, that belief system is totally inadequate to human needs, because every one of us faces life and every one of us faces death. This truth—that Jesus died and rose from the dead and became Lord both of the living and of the dead—liberates us from that bondage of self, of time, and of self-preoccupation.

We are not living to ourselves. We are living to Christ, and if we die, we die to Christ. He is there to receive us. We belong to Him. We have become God's responsibility. We don't have to carry the burden of arranging everything, providing everything, managing everything for ourselves. Our lives are the responsibility of the Lord.

In closing, let's look at the words of the psalmist David in Psalm 17, verse 15, who beautifully sums up this expectation.

As for me, I will behold thy face in righteousness: I shall be satisfied, when I awake, with thy likeness (KJV).

You see, there is hope that extends beyond the grave. David is saying, "I'll fall asleep in death. But there is a day coming, a moment coming, when I will awake. I will see His face. I will be clothed with His righteousness. And I will be satisfied."

Satisfied! What a powerful word that is. When I meditate on the Scripture we have just cited, I like to repeat it over and over to myself: "Satisfied... satisfied... fully satisfied. I will be satisfied."

That is my hope. It is my hope in life; and it is my hope in death. It is the hope that has liberated me from time and all its petty concerns and worries, liberated me from my own littleness, from my own inabilities—from my own weaknesses and frustrations. I am not shut up in that prison. What has liberated me? Hope! Oh, how I thank God for that hope!

WORDS OF HOPE

I hope you will want to join me in thanking the Lord for the hope that is so satisfying. But possibly, you may feel like the hopeless person I described earlier. Do you hear yourself saying, "It's no use?" Let me reassure you; you are not alone. When that was my condition, I cried out to God in my hopelessness and He met my need.

Would you like to pray together with me now? Let's go to God's Word together, and lift our prayer based upon the verse we studied earlier:

> *Father, I thank You for the promise of a hope that can liberate me. I want to receive it from You. I look to Your Word now, and in faith, I declare this truth: Your love is my source of hope. Hope comes to me through Jesus Christ. It is a gift to me by grace. Hope is eternal; and it will make me strong for holy living.*
>
> *Thank You, Lord, that as I say these words, You are breathing new hope into my heart. Thank You Lord, for this liberating hope. Amen.*

Chapter 4

HOPE IS PART OF SALVATION

IN THE PREVIOUS CHAPTERS, I HAVE BRIEFLY SHARED about my own personal battle with hopelessness. Even though I was a mature Christian and Bible teacher, I was not immune to this kind of suffering. So it comes as no surprise that many sincere Christians find themselves in the same desperate struggle today.

Hopelessness is one of the saddest conditions in human experience, but I believe it is possible to once again have genuine, biblical hope. Why? Because hope is part of our salvation in Jesus Christ! This will be our topic of this chapter's discussion, in which I will share with you from both the Scriptures and my experience.

SEVEN ESSENTIAL FACTS

By way of review, let's begin by briefly summarizing the seven scriptural facts we have already established. These truths are extremely important.

- First, there are three abiding realities in the Christian life: faith, hope, and love.

- Second, hope is produced by the new birth.

- Third, hope is based upon Christ's resurrection.

- Fourth, hope looks forward to Christ's return.

- Fifth, the source of hope is God's love.

- Sixth, hope motivates us to holy living.

- And seventh, hope transforms us into confident, radiant Christians.

A Surprising Truth

In this chapter, I will explain why hope is an essential part of our salvation. Most Christians of any denominational background have some kind of awareness that you cannot have salvation without faith. We are all familiar with the famous scriptural statement, "The just shall live by faith." That is perfectly true. However, it may come as a surprise to you that it is not the *whole* truth. What I want to emphasize in this chapter is that you cannot have salvation without hope as well. Hope is an essential part of salvation.

Here is what Paul says in Romans 8:24-25:

> *For in hope we have been saved* [or, by hope we have been saved], *but hope that is seen is not hope; for who hopes for what he already sees? But if we hope for what we do not see, with perseverance we wait eagerly for it.*

This verse reminds us of an important earlier point concerning the relationship between faith and hope. Faith is in the present, but hope turns toward the future. Here Paul is saying, *"In hope* [or by hope] *we have been saved."* In other words, hope does not take the place of faith—but it is an essential part of being saved. Without hope we do not have valid salvation.

Paul goes on to point out that hope produces perseverance. He says, *"If we hope for what we do not see, with perseverance we wait eagerly for it."* Perseverance, which we connected earlier with hope, is also an essential part of our salvation. Many passages of Scripture emphasize that we must persevere in our faith to the consummation of that faith. So hope, and with it, perseverance, is essential to salvation.

A MYSTERY DISCLOSED

This truth—that hope is essential to salvation—is clearly stated by Paul in another passage of his writings. I consider Colossians 1:25–27 to be one of the most beautiful and exciting passages of the New Testament! This is what Paul says:

> *I have become its servant* [the servant of the church] *by the commission God gave me to present to you the word of God in its fullness—the mystery that has been kept hidden for ages and generations, but is now disclosed to the Lord's people* [the saints]. *To them God has chosen to*

make known among the Gentiles the glorious riches of this mystery, which is Christ in you, the hope of glory (NIV).

Let's repeat that last verse for emphasis:

To them God has chosen to make known among the Gentiles the glorious riches of this mystery, which is Christ in you, the hope of glory (NIV).

In this passage, Paul is telling us that he was commissioned by God to present to His people (the church) the Word of God in its fullness. Then he goes on to explain what the fullness of the Word of God means. Paul says that *the full presentation of the truth* of God's Word involves a "*mystery*," which "*has been kept hidden for ages and generations.*"

At the time of the New Testament, the Greek word "mystery" had a special meaning. There were certain "mystery religions" into which people were initiated through secret rites. Only people who had been through the secret rites and initiation would be allowed to enter into these religions. So Paul's use of the word "mystery" does not mean something which can never be understood. More exactly, it means something which can be understood only by the initiated—those who have met the condition for entering into this understanding.

By using this term, Paul is revealing that the Christian faith contains a mystery—something that has been kept hidden for ages and generations. All the great men of old, all the great philosophers, all the wise men, all the kings and conquerors, never knew this mystery. It was reserved for us in this present age. Paul says what has been hidden is now disclosed to the saints.

Doesn't that make you feel excited? Are we not privileged to be among those to whom this mystery—which was never before revealed, even to the wisest of men—is now disclosed?

THREE SHORT WORDS

God wants "*to make known among the Gentiles the glorious riches of this mystery.*" More literally in Greek, "The riches of the glory of this mystery." Paul almost runs out of words trying to explain how exciting this mystery is. What is the mystery?

The answer to this question is not presented in some extensive philosophical treatise with long, complicated words that most people can't understand. I was a professional philosopher, so I especially appreciate the simplicity of the Scriptures. I remember reading the works of the philosopher Emmanuel Kant, where one sentence would sometimes extend for two pages without a period. Thankfully, that is not the way the Bible reveals mysteries.

This glorious mystery is revealed in three short words: *Christ in you*.

That is the most exciting truth that can ever be revealed to humanity! That Christ, the eternal Son of God, by the Holy Spirit, can be in us. In us as individuals; among us as the people of God. This is the hope of glory.

What is the hope of glory? *Christ in you. Christ in me.* This is the secret—the mystery which God has reserved for us. Don't you feel privileged? Don't you get excited when you think about that? Are you able to realize what it means to have Christ in you? It means you have the hope of glory.

There is a future. The one who has Christ in him has hope for that future—a glorious, radiant, confident expectation of eternal glory with almighty God, the holy angels, and the redeemed of all ages—from age to age. That is what you have when you have Christ in you, the hope of glory.

ONLY TWO POSSIBILITIES

What about those who do not have Christ in them? It is quite a contrast to what this glorious mystery means to us as believers. Let's look at Paul's vivid description of the condition of those who are outside of Christ. In Ephesians 2:11-12, writing to those who are Gentiles, Paul reminds them not to forget what life was like without Christ.

> *Therefore, remember that formerly you who are Gentiles by birth and called "uncircumcised" by those who call themselves "the circumcision" (which is done in the body by human hands)— remember that at that time you were separate from Christ, excluded from citizenship in Israel and foreigners to the covenants of the promise, without hope and without God in the world* (NIV).

Please pay close attention to that awful list of negatives. What cruel words they are! *"Separate from Christ; excluded from citizenship in Israel and foreigners to the covenants of the promise."* (Have you ever lived as a foreigner in a land that was not yours? I have, and I know what it is like to be a foreigner. You never feel that you really belong.) That is what Paul is saying about those who are without Christ—they are foreigners; they don't belong. But the last two phrases are the most tragic: "*without hope and without God.*"

Allow me to repeat those phrases. I want to burn them into your thinking. Maybe you are in this category—the condition they describe. If so, you need to pay attention to them all the more carefully.

- Separate from Christ
- Excluded from citizenship in Israel
- Foreigners to the covenants of the promise
- Without hope
- Without God in the world

For every person, there are just two possible conditions for your life. If you have Christ in you, you have the hope of glory. But if you are without Christ, then you are without hope and without God.

THE NECESSITY OF HOPE

Now we can see why it is so critical to know that hope is a part of our salvation! Without hope, we don't have Christ. Without Christ, we don't have salvation.

Hope is not just an appendage to salvation. It is an essential part of salvation. We are saved in hope, and we are saved by hope. Hope is built on the faith that brings salvation—but it is also an essential part of the total package. If we do not have this hope, then we are without Christ. And if we are without Christ, we are without God. We are foreigners. We are excluded. We are separate. We are hopeless. What a terrible condition to be in!

Thanks be to God—it is not necessary for anyone who hears this message to remain in that condition. If you will turn your life over to God and receive Jesus, then you will not be without Christ. Then you will very quickly know what it means to have in you the hope of glory. May the Lord help each one of us to be sure about our salvation.

AN OPEN HEART

What about you? As you have been reading these words, does it produce a desire in you to confirm that you have Christ in you? Do you want to make sure you have this "hope of glory" we have been talking about?

It may be that you have not yet made the decision to receive Jesus Christ and the hope He brings. Or, you may have made that decision, but would like to confirm it and receive the hope Jesus promises.

Whatever your situation, you can come with certainty into this glorious hope by praying the following words:

> *Dear Lord Jesus, I want to receive You fully into my life right now. Come into me, and flood my entire being with Your hope—the hope of glory. I open my heart to You now, more fully than I ever have before. Thank You that You have come into me—making it so that I will never again be without hope and without God in the world. In Jesus' name. Amen.*

Chapter 5

HOPE GROWS STRONG THROUGH TESTING

Throughout my lifetime, I have been privileged to pray for thousands of Christians facing all kinds of challenges in their lives. Although the issues have varied from person to person, there is one problem that seems to be universal. At some point in our lives, most of us—if not all of us—experience hopelessness.

As Christians, we may have to contend with hopelessness. But we don't ever have to succumb to it! Even so, sometimes we feel as if we are losing this age-old battle. How do we handle that challenge? This will be the topic of discussion in this chapter.

EXULTING IN TRIBULATIONS

We have seen that hope, like faith, is an essential aspect of our salvation. Just as faith grows through testing, in a similar way our hope is increased and matured as we go through various trials and tests.

What happens when our hope is tested? To answer that question, let's first look at Romans 5:1–5:

> *Therefore, having been justified by faith* [justified means acquitted, made righteous], *we have peace with God through our Lord Jesus Christ, through whom also we have obtained our introduction by faith into this grace in which we stand; and we exult in hope of the glory of God* (Romans 5:1–2).

Paul says that we *"exult in hope of the glory of God."* The word "exult" means to rejoice, to be very confident. Notice that it is hope that produces that joy and confidence, even to the point of boasting. But that is not all Paul has to say. He continues in the next verse:

> *And not only this, but we also exult in our trib-*
> *ulations* (Romans 5:3).

In this verse, Paul says something quite different from the previous verse. We can understand exulting in hope. But how do we exult in tribulations, trials, and testings? Maybe you have never thought about this possibility. How do you react to tribulation? Do you exult in it?

Why should we exult in our tribulations? Paul goes on to explain:

> *Knowing that tribulation brings about perse-*
> *verance; and perseverance, proven character;*
> *and proven character, hope; and hope does not*
> *disappoint, because the love of God has been*
> *poured out within our hearts through the Holy*
> *Spirit who was given to us* (Romans 5:3–5).

In these verses, Paul is pointing to a progression that leads to hope. When we come into tribulation, if we hold on to our faith, then we can hold on to our hope. What tribulation does in us is to initiate a process which is essential for the building of Christian character. The end result is that through tribulation, God gives us a strong, stable, confident hope.

You see, hope has to be tested by tribulation in order to be proved genuine and become strong. Notice the progression: tribulation produces perseverance; perseverance produces proven character; and proven character produces a hope that is not disappointed.

WHAT TRIBULATION PRODUCES

Let me tell you something about perseverance. Do you know the key to perseverance? It is to persevere! There is just no other way to learn perseverance but to persevere. It is like swimming. You can have all of the theories on how to swim. You can picture all the strokes and motions in your mind. You can know all the facts about breathing properly. But ultimately, the only way to learn to swim is *to swim*. Likewise, the only way to learn to persevere is to persevere.

When we come into tribulation—and we surely will—we need to hold on to one important truth: the trial we are facing is for our good. It is helping us. God is permitting us to go through this particular trial because it is the only way to produce what is needed in us for that final strong, confident, radiant, unshakable hope. Tribulation produces perseverance.

What does perseverance produce? It produces proven character. A person who has been through tribulation and comes out victorious has proven character. Paul says that *"we are more than conquerors through him who loved us"* (Romans 8:37 NIV). What does it mean to be "more than conquerors?" I understand it this way: you come out of tribulation with more than you had when you went into it. As a conqueror, you do not just hold your own—you gain a victory. That is how it is when we persevere in tribulation—we come out with proven character.

Proven character is essential because it establishes our hope. We had the hope of the glory of God before our trial started. But when we come out of it, we have an altogether different degree of hope. This tried and tested hope does not disappoint us, but opens us up to the fullness of God's love.

You see, to receive the fullness of God's love, you have to have proven character. You have to have stability. Your life and personality have to be a vessel strong enough and large enough to contain all the love that God wants to pour into you.

DOOR OF HOPE

I would like to illustrate this process from a passage in the prophets of the Old Testament. In Hosea, chapter 2, God is telling Israel how He is going to deal with them. Surprisingly, He speaks about bringing them into a time of tribulation. But then He says:

> *There I will give her back her vineyards, and will make the Valley of Achor a door of hope* (Hosea 2:15 NIV).

It is important to know that the word *achor* means "trouble." Here is what the Lord is saying: "I'll let Israel come into trouble, but I will work through that trouble so that it actually will become the door of hope." This is a wonderful biblical principle. Remember, whenever God brings us into trouble, He will provide a way out when we pass through it. There will be an exit point, and it is the door of hope.

THE WORD OF GOD

I want to explain briefly two further requirements for cultivating the kind of strong, confident hope that we are discussing. The first requirement is that we need to give heed to the Scriptures—to accept everything the Bible says. Paul states this in Romans 15:4:

> *For whatever was written in earlier times was written for our instruction* [Paul is talking about the Scriptures; all Scripture is written for our instruction. What was the purpose?] *so that through perseverance and the encouragement of the Scriptures we might have hope.*

We have already pointed out that perseverance is essential for us to cultivate this kind of hope. But Paul is saying we also need the encouragement of the Scriptures. When you are in tribulation and when you are having a hard time, turn to the Scriptures. Read them! Believe them! They will encourage you; they will strengthen your hope. Do not deny yourself this wonderful, God-given source of hope, which is in the Scriptures.

Sometimes you might not feel like reading the Bible. But just make up your mind. Tell yourself, "I'm going to read the Bible until I hear from God. I'm going to read until I get something out of it that strengthens my hope and gives me the grace to go on persevering." Remember, that is one of the purposes of the Bible—to instruct us, that through the Word we might have hope.

By the Power of the Holy Spirit

The second requirement is a reliance upon the Holy Spirit. Hope can only come to us in its fullness through the supernatural power of the Holy Spirit. We see this a little further on in the fifteenth chapter of Romans. In verse 13, Paul gives us these beautiful words:

> *Now may the God of hope fill you with all joy and peace in believing, so that you will abound in hope by the power of the Holy Spirit.*

Think of what that means to be filled with all joy and peace in believing. What is the result? An abundance of hope. God wants to fill us with all joy and peace, so that we may "abound in hope." That means having more than just enough hope for ourselves. It means having enough hope to minister to others as well. When others are downcast, we have a word of hope, a word of encouragement for them. But please notice, it is by the power of the Holy Spirit. We cannot do this on our own. We must open ourselves fully to the Holy Spirit. The Spirit of God is the only agent who can minister this kind of victorious hope in our lives.

THE GOD OF HOPE

I would like to close this chapter with the beautiful phrase with which Paul begins Romans 15:13: *"Now may the God of hope fill you."*

Do you realize that the Lord is the God of hope? He is not merely the God of peace, the God of joy, the God of righteousness, and the God of power, but He is also the God of hope. You cannot know God without having hope.

As we close this chapter, let's read again what the entire verse says:

> *May the God of hope fill you with all joy and peace in believing, so that you will abound in hope by the power of the Holy Spirit* (Romans 15:13).

When you and I are filled, here is the result: we *abound in hope.* Hope bubbles up and overflows within you and me. This is my sincere prayer for you—*that you may abound in hope by the power of the Holy Spirit.* Consider these words. Meditate on them. When you find yourself in a troubling situation or facing affliction, turn back to them. Declare them again, over and over, until they become completely real in your life and your experience.

Chapter 6

HOPE IN THIS LIFE

OFTEN, WE DON'T APPRECIATE THE IMPORTANT THINGS in life until we lose them. Isn't that true? It is especially true when it comes to hope. In my own experience, it wasn't until I lost all hope that I realized how much I desperately needed it. If that has ever happened to you, you know how serious the condition of hopelessness can be. Our very lives depend upon having some semblance of hope.

When I cried out to God in my state of hopelessness, He met my need through the power of the Holy Spirit. If you are struggling with hopelessness right now, don't give up! What God did for me, He will do for you as well. He has promised to answer all who call upon Him for help.

NINE ASPECTS OF HOPE

In this chapter, I want to deal with the topic of hope in this life. Before we begin, however, I would like to once again list the nine facts about hope we have learned up to this point. As you read through this list, please notice that we are *not* talking about the kind of hope that is often spoken of in this world. That kind of hope is merely wishful thinking. It's nice, but it won't get you very far.

The hope we are talking about is so much more powerful than wishful thinking. It is God-centered! It is Christ-centered! Our hope looks back to Christ's death and resurrection, and looks forward to Christ's coming. It sees every intervening situation in our lives in the light of those two great events. As you read this list, think of some of the circumstances you presently face—and place those situations from your own life under the spotlight of this kind of hope.

So far in this book we have considered nine facts about hope:

- First, there are three abiding realities in the Christian life—faith, hope, and love.

- Second, hope is produced by the new birth.

- Third, hope is based on Christ's resurrection.

- Fourth, hope looks forward to Christ's return.

- Fifth, hope's source is God's love.

- Sixth, hope motivates us to holy living.

- Seventh, hope transforms us into radiant Christians.

- Eighth, hope is an essential part of salvation.

- Finally, hope grows through testing.

THE ULTIMATE BASIS

As we focus in this chapter on how hope relates to this life—that is, within the time frame of life on this earth—it is important to remember that all true hope is based on faith. And all true faith, in turn, is based on Scripture.

Therefore, if we are going to have *real* hope in this life, we need a scriptural basis for that hope.

The question I'm going to ask you now may come as a surprise to you. Did you know that there is one scriptural basis which is fully sufficient for every situation and every need? If I searched the scriptures I could find many others, but for our purposes here I would like to focus on just this one scriptural basis for persistent hope and optimism. It is Romans chapter 8, verse 28:

> *And we know that God causes all things to work*
> *together for good to those who love God, to those*
> *who are called according to His purpose.*

Let me draw your attention to the first three words of that verse—*and we know.* The most important question you and I need to ask ourselves, right from the start, is this: *Do we really know?* Do I really know that God causes all things to work together for good to those who love God?

This means that there is nothing that has ever happened, or ever will happen, that is not covered by what is stated in this scripture. There is no event, no situation; there is no disaster in which we need to despair. Why?

Because God causes everything—even apparent disasters—to work together for good to those who love Him.

God is in supreme control. He sits on the throne of the universe. He has never abdicated, and He is never going to abdicate. All power in heaven and in earth has been given to the Lord Jesus Christ. God the Father and God the Son are on our side. "*If God be for us, who can be against us?*" (Romans 8:31 KJV).

Two Conditions

However, before we dig deeper into this verse (Romans 8:28) as the basis of our Christian optimism, there is something you and I need to do. We need to make sure we are fulfilling the conditions stated in that verse.

What are the conditions? We find them as we look at the verse again. Paul writes, "*God causes all things to work together for good to those who love God, to those who are called according to his purpose.*" Those are the two requirements we must meet before we can say, "This is my basis for optimism." First, we have to be sure that we truly love God. Second, we must know that we are walking in the purpose to which He has called us.

These two conditions are very important. You see, God has a purpose for each life. All that He does in our lives—His gifts, His provision, His leading, His watchful care—everything He has done for us is for the fulfillment of that purpose. However, if we are rejecting God's purpose, if we are walking contrary to God's purpose, if we are seeking to do something other than His calling—then that Scripture doesn't truly apply to us. In order to rectify the situation so it will apply, we have to repent. We have to turn back and get in line with God's purpose for our lives *before* we can claim that Scripture.

Having done that, for all of us who truly love God and are sincerely walking in the purpose to which God has called us, then that Scripture gives you and me a base for total, never-failing optimism! Nothing can ever happen that should cause us to despair, because God is working everything together for your good and for mine.

Confident in His Goodness

I think also of the beautiful words of David in Psalm 27:13, words which I dearly love.

*I would have despaired unless I had believed
that I would see the goodness of the Lord in the
land of the living.*

The New International Version of this verse says:

*I remain confident of this: I will see the goodness
of the Lord in the land of the living.*

Both translations are beautiful, but personally, I like to combine them:

> I decline to despair because I do believe that
> I will see the goodness of the Lord in the
> land of the living, and I am very confident
> that I will see the goodness of the Lord in
> the land of the living.

I can meet every situation that arises with this strong buoyant hope: *God is working it together for my good*. It may not always appear that way at first. I can assure you, in the course of all my years as a Christian, I have encountered many situations and passed through many circumstances where it seemed that everything was against me. But, thank God, by experience I learned not to despair, nor to give way, nor to look solely at the outward appearance of a situation. I learned to see it through the eyes of God and the light of Scripture. I knew that somewhere behind those dark clouds, the hand of Almighty God is working everything together for my good—shaping me, molding me, leading me forward.

I learned that His working in my life was not primarily for my enjoyment, but for my good. God is more concerned for you and me to be "good" than "happy." If my happiness is consistent with my goodness, that is wonderful. But if at any time it is necessary for me to be unhappy that it may produce goodness in me, then God will always go for the goodness—and sacrifice *temporarily* the happiness. In His wisdom, He knows that the happiness will come back later, when His purposes have been accomplished. Over many years, I have learned to trust His wisdom, and so can you.

THE CROSS

As we continue with this theme of how hope relates to this life—within the time frame of life on this earth—there is one truth we always need to bear in mind: At the center of God's provision for His people is the cross.

When it comes to having hope, understanding and believing this truth makes all the difference. If we get away from the cross, then we get away from that sure, unfailing certainty which gives us the kind of hope the Scripture speaks about. Please notice what Paul says of God in Romans 8:32:

> *He who did not spare His own Son, but delivered Him over for us all, how will He not also with Him freely give us all things?*

Here is the remarkable measure of God's love and commitment to us: He did not spare his own Son, the Lord Jesus Christ. Paul states this very logically, "If God didn't spare Jesus, then there is nothing good that He will withhold from us." That includes hope.

As Paul continues to expound this principle, he uses such beautiful language!

> *How will he not also with Him* [notice, it must be with Him] *freely give us all things?*

Again, everything—including hope—is included! If we keep the cross central in our lives, then we can go on and affirm what follows in the rest of that chapter. Please take some time to meditate on these glorious words in Romans 8:35–39:

Who will separate us from the love of Christ? Will tribulation, or distress, or persecution, or famine, or nakedness, or peril, or sword? Just as it is written, "For Your sake we are being put to death all day long; we were considered as sheep to be slaughtered." But in all these things we overwhelmingly conquer through Him who loved us. For I am convinced that neither death, nor life, nor angels, nor principalities, nor things present, nor things to come, nor powers, nor height, nor depth, nor any other created thing, will be able to separate us from the love of God, which is in Christ Jesus our Lord.

What a wonderful confidence we can have! What a deep assurance that the love of God surrounds our lives!

WHATEVER HAPPENS

Please notice, however, that our assurance of God's love and care does not depend on everything going right. Paul talks about tribulation, distress, persecution, famine, nakedness, peril, and sword. He says we are counted as sheep for the slaughter. But in all of that, he still says *we overwhelmingly conquer!* Why? Because God is on our side. Because God is working out His purposes through all these difficulties. Because we know that, no matter what the appearances are, no matter what the situation is, God is working all things together for good to those who love him, to those who are called according to his purpose.

In our understanding of God loving us through every situation we face, we cannot let our eyes wander from the cross and from the purpose of God in our lives. We cannot let the pressures of life distract us from the truths that are basic, fundamental, and central to our faith: the cross, the love of God, the commitment of God to us, the faithfulness of God, the fact that He has called us, the fact that He has a special purpose in life for each of us. If we are walking in line with that purpose, God is going to see to it that His special plans for our lives are totally fulfilled.

Then we can say with David, "I remain confident of this: I will see the goodness of the Lord in the land of the living." Or, we can say the other version, "I would have despaired unless I had believed that I would see the goodness of the Lord in the land of the living." Whichever version we chose, we will see the goodness of the Lord in the land of the living! We will have hope in this life.

Settling the Issue

There is much we have covered in this chapter on *Hope in this Life.* As you have read these words, however, there may be some doubt lingering in your mind. Is there an issue still troubling you?

Perhaps you aren't sure that you are meeting the two conditions I described earlier: to truly love God and to be walking in His purposes for your life. Sometimes we are certain we love God, but uncertain that we are following in His will. Other times, it's the other way around—we are earnestly serving Him, but we feel that our hearts, for some reason, have grown cold. Let's settle these or any other issues that may have arisen in your mind and heart by praying the following prayer together:

> *Dear Lord Jesus, You know my heart better than I do. I want to follow You, but I am struggling in a few specific areas. (Name what comes to your mind now.) I know You love me, and that You died for me on the cross. Lord, I place my belief and trust in You now, and I commit myself to follow You with my whole heart. Thank You for Your grace to*

do Your will. I place my life in Your hands, Lord. Amen.

Chapter 7

HOPE IN DEATH

THE TITLE OF THIS CHAPTER, "HOPE IN DEATH," MAY strike some as a little strange. For many readers, it could represent a complete paradox—the impossibility of "Hope in Death." In a verse we considered earlier, Paul spoke of those who were *"separate from Christ, excluded...having no hope and without God in the world"* (Ephesians 2:12). Sadly, we all know people who have no such hope, and who would find it nearly impossible to have "hope in death."

However, we learned in the previous chapter that if we are in Christ, we have a basis for *never-failing optimism!* No matter what happens, no matter what the outward appearances, no matter what the situation, if we love God and are walking in accordance with His purpose and calling for our life, then He causes everything that happens to us to work together for good. It may not appear so at the time, but it will work out that way. And so we can say as David said in Psalm 27:13:

> *I remain confident of this: I will see the goodness*
> *of the Lord in the land of the living* (NIV).

AN INESCAPABLE APPOINTMENT

I want to take the theme of hope one step further, beyond the time frame of life on this earth. In this chapter I will be sharing with you about "Hope in Death."

First, we all need to face the fact that at some time we are going to die—unless the Lord Jesus returns first. Realistically, you and I must face the fact that death is an appointment for all of us. It is one appointment that we will not fail to keep.

The writer of Hebrews states this very clearly in chapter 9, verse 27:

> *And inasmuch as it is appointed for men to die*
> *once and after this comes judgment.*

Please notice that word "appointed." It refers to *an appointment*. You and I may miss every appointment we make on earth. You and I may never turn up at the right time or the right place. But *this* appointment you and I will keep. It is an appointment with death.

Bear in mind, however, that death is not the end. We do not cease to exist; we simply pass out of this world into another mode of existence. There is something beyond death—it is the judgment of God. "*It is appointed for men to die once, and after this comes judgment.*" We all are going to experience that moment when we will have to answer to Almighty God for the lives we have led. At that time, the primary question we will have to answer is this: Have I responded affirmatively to the gospel of Jesus Christ?

I have regularly asserted that any religion which offers hope only for this life cannot meet man's deepest need. To my understanding, Christianity is the only faith that has a real and positive answer to man's need concerning death. Why? Because only the Christian gospel offers hope beyond the grave.

Paul expresses this in very vivid terms in First Corinthians 15:19:

If only for this life we have hope in Christ, we are of all people most to be pitied (NIV).

If our Christian faith were only for this life, then we would be the most pitiful of all people on the earth. We would be self-deluded. We would be walking in a dream. We would be living in a fantasy land. The truth of the matter is that faith in Christ takes us through death, through the portals of the grave, and into an eternal life with Christ in the next world.

GLIMPSES FROM THE OLD TESTAMENT

It is irrefutable that the Bible specifically offers hope in death—not only in the New Testament, but also in the Old Testament. Does that surprise you? Many people have said to me, "The Old Testament doesn't say anything about life after death." But that is a complete misconception. There are many passages in the Old Testament which specifically speak about life after death, and even portray the kind of experience some people will have in the next world.

Let's take a brief moment to look at three of these passages.

Perhaps one of the clearest statements in the Old Testament about eternal life, and the resurrection of the dead, is given to us by the prophet Daniel:

> *Many of those who sleep in the dust of the ground will awake, these to everlasting life, but the others to disgrace and everlasting contempt* (Daniel 12:2).

Then there are two statements from the book of Proverbs, beginning with chapter 11, verse 4:

> *Wealth is worthless in the day of wrath, but righteousness delivers from death* (NIV).

You can spend your life piling up money and wealth. But as everybody knows, you cannot take it with you. Death is the end of all that. Whatever benefit your wealth afforded you in life, it will do you no good whatever in death. On the other hand, the proverb says *righteousness delivers from death.* Righteousness is a way of escape from the bitterness and the crushing burden of death. Shouldn't more people be paying attention to this truth?

The same sentiment is stated in Proverbs 14:32:

When calamity comes, the wicked are brought down, but even in death the righteous seek refuge in God (NIV).

Another translation of this verse says the righteous "have confidence," or "have hope." Notice again, *"When calamity comes, the wicked are brought down."* The wicked have no answer for calamity. It snuffs them out and finishes them off as far as this life is concerned. But even in death, the righteous have a refuge.

LIGHT OF THE NEW TESTAMENT

Let's now look to the New Testament to see what it has to say about the refuge the righteous have in their death. What the Old Testament states briefly concerning hope in death is brought fully out into the open, in the light of the New Testament.

In Second Timothy 1:9-10, Paul speaks about the grace that we receive through faith in Jesus Christ. He emphasizes to us that this grace did not begin in time, but that it is eternal. It was in the mind of God before creation ever took place. This is what he says, in very vivid and powerful words:

> *This grace was given us in Christ Jesus before the beginning of time, but it has now been revealed through the appearing of our Savior, Christ Jesus, who has destroyed death and has brought life and immortality to light through the gospel* (NIV).

Those beautiful words of Paul help you and me to know that we are not an accident looking for somewhere to happen. You and I are part of God's eternal plan. Before the world was created He knew you—He knew your name. He had a plan for your life. Once He had chosen you in Christ, He gave you the grace that would be needed for you to fulfill His eternal plan for your life.

However, God's plan was not revealed until Jesus came. Jesus, by His own death and resurrection, "*has destroyed death and has brought life and immortality to light through the gospel.*" Isn't that a beautiful phrase? The word "gospel" means "good news." This is surely good news! What a life-changing encouragement to know that Jesus Christ, on our behalf, has destroyed death. In place of death, He has made life and immortality available to everyone who believes.

THE HOPE THAT IS OURS

This "good news" is more fully unfolded by Paul in First Thessalonians 4:13–18. We will consider this important passage verse by verse, beginning in verse 13:

> *Brothers and sisters, we do not want you to be uninformed about those who sleep in death, so that you do not grieve like the rest of mankind, who have no hope* (NIV).

This verse echoes a verse we read previously (Ephesians 2:11-12) which also speaks of "*those who have no hope, who are without Christ.*" What tragic words those are! Did you know that the Bible speaks about death as "falling asleep" only if it is referring to the death of a believer? The meaning is clear. He or she may have "fallen asleep," but they are going to awaken. In the next verse Paul gives the reason why we do not need to grieve like those who have no hope:

> *For we believe that Jesus died and rose again, and so we believe that God will bring with Jesus those who have fallen asleep in him* (1 Thessalonians 4:14 NIV).

The resurrection of Christ is the guarantee of our resurrection if we are believers in Him. We are identified with Him in death, in burial, and in glorious resurrection. In verse 15, Paul continues:

> *According to the Lord's word, we tell you that we who are still alive, who are left until the coming of the Lord, will certainly not precede those who have fallen asleep* (1 Thessalonians 4:15 NIV).

Let me clarify what Paul is saying: Those believers who are alive on earth when the Lord returns will not meet the Lord any sooner than those who have already died, because those who have died will be resurrected first. Then both the living and those who have died will be caught up to meet the Lord together.

THREE GLORIOUS SOUNDS

Paul brings all of this to its culmination in the next three verses. Let's begin with verse 16:

> *For the Lord himself will come down from heaven, with a loud command, with the voice of the archangel and with the trumpet call of God* (NIV).

Three glorious sounds are going to be heard at that instant! First will be the Lord's "loud command." This is referring to the command of the Lord Jesus to the believing dead to come out of their graves. You see, when Jesus gave that one command to Lazarus to come out of the grave, Lazarus came out, but Jesus had to name him specifically. He said, "Lazarus, come out." Because if Jesus had not named him specifically, but simply said, "Come out," *all* the dead would have come out! When Jesus returns, it will be different. He is going to call forth out of the dead all those who have died in Him. That will be His loud command.

The second sound will be the voice of the archangel calling the whole creation to attend to what God is doing. Finally, there will be the trumpet call of God. In the Bible, one of the purposes of a trumpet call is to gather God's people together for a solemn meeting, which in this case will be the meeting of God's people in the air with Jesus.

So there is the command of the Lord, the voice of the archangel, and the trumpet call of God. What happens next?

The dead in Christ will rise first. After that, we who are still alive and are left will be caught

*up together with them in the clouds to meet the
Lord in the air. And so we will be with the Lord
forever* (1 Thessalonians 4:16–17 NIV).

I like that word "forever." It means there will be no more
separation from the presence of the Lord, or from our dear
ones. If you have ever stood at the deathbed of a loved one
who knows the Lord, there is a parting. There is a sadness,
and there is a grief. I have experienced that in my own life.
But I know that such moments are not a final parting.
They are only for a time. There will be a reunion! We will
be reunited with the Lord. When we are being reunited
with the Lord, we will be reunited with one another.

You see, there is such awful heaviness, such awful bitterness in the death of those who do not know the Lord.
But there is such wonderful assurance and peace in the
death and passing of those who do. That is why Paul con-
cludes by saying in First Thessalonians 4:18, "*Therefore
encourage one another with these words*" (NIV).

These are days in which we need encouraging words.
As we close this chapter, let me encourage you with those
words of hope. If you know Jesus, death is not the end. In
reality, it is the doorway into a new and glorious eternity.
You will not forever be separated from the loved ones who

know Him. We shall all be reunited with the Lord and with one another. *"And so we will be with the Lord forever."* If that isn't reason enough for us to have great hope, even in the face of death, I don't know what is.

Chapter 8

HOPE FOR CREATION

IN THE TWO PREVIOUS CHAPTERS WE CONSIDERED what the Bible has to say about hope in two successive phases of human experience. First, hope during life in this world. Second, hope in death.

Perhaps you are a mature and faithful Christian, but you find yourself in a baffling struggle to live in hope. I know that battle, because I fought it myself. So I want to begin this chapter with a clear statement about hope, grounded in the teaching of the written Word of God:

We who are committed to Jesus Christ, walking in His purposes, can have hope. *You and I can have hope.*

First of all, we can have hope in this life because God is making *everything* work together for good. This is what He has promised in His Word: *"And we know that God causes all things to work together for good to those who love God, to those who are called according to His purpose"* (Romans 8:28).

This means that no matter what the appearances are, no matter what the situation is, the hand of God is in it. He is making *everything* work together for good, if we love Him and are walking in His purposes.

Second, our hope does not end in this world. Paul says in First Corinthians 15:19:

> *If only for this life we have hope in Christ, we are of all people most to be pitied* (NIV).

If our faith does not meet the challenge of death, it is a worthless faith. It is a deception. But thank God, it does. We have hope—not only in this life, but also in death.

As I have stated previously, this is not wishful thinking or fantasy. The biblical basis for all true hope is the resurrection of Jesus Christ. On this basis, the Bible offers us solid grounds for hope in this life, in death, and beyond the grave.

THORNS AND THISTLES

In this chapter, I am going to broaden our theme still further. We are going to consider hope for creation—for the whole of creation.

First of all, we need to understand that Adam's rebellion and fall did not only affect all of Adam's descendants (meaning, the entire human race). Adam's fall also affected the whole area of creation over which God had given Adam both authority and responsibility to rule as God's vice regent. This is a very important point. Why? Because we cannot understand the state of reality in the world today unless we realize that Adam's fall had a negative effect on the whole created order, over which he was ruler, for which he was answerable to God.

Adam's sin admitted a negative, blighting influence that affected both the animal and plant kingdoms. Every aspect of creation on this earth was adversely affected by Adam's fall. We see a small picture of this in the words that the Lord spoke to Adam when He challenged him with the results of his disobedience, in Genesis 3:17-18:

To Adam he [the Lord] *said, "Because you listened to your wife and ate fruit from the tree about which I commanded you, 'You must not eat from it,' cursed is the ground because of you; through painful toil you will eat food from it all the days of your life. It* [the ground] *will produce thorns and thistles for you"* (NIV).

The ground was cursed because of Adam's sin. Thorns and thistles were not the way God intended plants to grow. They are the result of the negative influence and impairment that came through Adam's disobedience. It affected the whole creation. Every time you see thorns and thistles, just say to yourself, "Those are the evidences that the earth is under a curse."

LONGING FOR REDEMPTION

In Romans 8:18–23, Paul gives us a dramatic description of what is happening in creation at the present moment:

I consider that our present sufferings are not worth comparing with the glory that will be revealed in us. For the creation waits in eager expectation for the children of God to be revealed. [This is the redemption of God's believing people.] *For the creation was subjected to frustration* [other translations read "vanity" or "futility"], *not by its own choice, but by the will of the one who subjected it, in hope that the creation itself will be liberated from its bondage to decay and brought into the freedom and glory of the children of God. We know that the whole creation has been groaning as in the pains of childbirth right up to the present time. Not only so, but we ourselves, who have the firstfruits of the Spirit, groan inwardly as we wait eagerly for our adoption to sonship, the redemption of our bodies* (NIV).

Notice the succession of words that give evidence to the curse: *sufferings, frustration, bondage, decay, groaning, pains.* You see, the tragic fall of the first Adam brought a blight—not only on himself and his descendants, but also on the whole creation. However, the total redemption achieved by Jesus, the last Adam, extends not only to Adam and his descendants, but also to all of creation. Therefore, when man is redeemed, creation will also be redeemed together with man.

In this present age, however, believers share in that wordless longing of all creation for the hour of redemption. Paul is saying, "Not only is creation groaning as in the pains of childbirth right up to the present time. We ourselves, who have the first fruits of the Spirit, groan inwardly as we wait eagerly for our adoption as sons, the redemption of our bodies."

What does Paul mean by "the first fruits of the Spirit"? He is referring to the revelation of the Holy Spirit within us that enables us to see beneath the surface, to see what is really going on in the spiritual realm.

So, creation is groaning, waiting for that glorious day, and we who have the first fruits of the Spirit are also groaning. We are looking for a birth of a new age which will be the redemption of man and the redemption of the earth which was blighted and cursed through man's fall.

ALL CREATION YEARNS

This anticipation and expectation of nature for redemption—even as man is redeemed—is beautifully portrayed by the psalmist in Psalm 96:11–13:

> *Let the heavens rejoice, let the earth be glad;*
> *let the sea resound, and all that is in it. Let*

*the fields be jubilant, and everything in them;
let all the trees of the forest sing for joy. Let all
creation rejoice before the Lord, for he comes, he
comes to judge the earth. He will judge the world
in righteousness and the peoples in his faithfulness* (NIV).

In this vivid picture, all creation is waiting for the coming of the Lord to bring redemption to man and to earth.
By way of explaining that more fully, I want to quote a section from my book, *Through the Psalms*. It is a comment
on those verses of the psalmist.

Awaiting the Climax

> *The creation waits in eager expectation for the
> children of God to be revealed. For the creation
> was subjected to frustration, not by its own
> choice* (Romans 8:19–20 NIV).

Man by his rebellion against his Creator
brought corruption and decay upon the
whole natural world around him. That
which was blighted through his fall can be
restored only through his redemption. This
is the climax that all nature awaits. Too often

man himself loses sight of this, but the anticipation of nature grows stronger all the time.

With insight given by the Holy Spirit, the psalmist here interprets the wordless longing of the natural world around him. In his spirit he senses a hushed anticipation, like the stillness in a concert auditorium as the conductor with upraised baton surveys his orchestra to make sure that each player is ready for the opening note. Heaven above and earth beneath, seas and fields and trees, all await the coming of the Lord to restore to them what was lost through man's fall. At that moment, like the orchestra as the baton descends, they will break forth into a symphony of praise and jubilation.

How about you and me? Are we as ready as nature is for that great climax? May God grant that you and I be more expectant and excited than the trees and the fields and the seas and the heavens!

In this book, *Through the Psalms,* every one of these meditations on the Psalms is followed by what I entitle *Faith's Response*. If we accept the truth presented, we should respond, in turn, to the Lord. Here is *Faith's Response* to the words of the psalmist, and to the truth which we are embracing.

> By Your Spirit, Lord, keep me in continual
> excited anticipation of Your coming.

Paul says that if we have the first fruits of the Holy Spirit within us, we will identify with the groaning and anticipation of nature. Nature is waiting for the manifestation of its creator, the Lord's return in glory. Everything is going to break forth into a glorious symphony of worship, praise, and thanksgiving. Everything in nature is making itself ready!

How about you and me? Shouldn't we be more ready for the Lord's return than nature? Shouldn't we be more excited? Since we can read the Bible and study the truths of Scripture, shouldn't we be "on tiptoe" of expectation, as the J.B. Phillips translation says? You see, we are in the midst of the birth pangs of a new age. We can groan now, but we have a sure and certain hope that a new age is going to be born.

In light of that, let's take a moment now to offer this faith response to the Lord:

By Your Spirit, Lord, keep me in continual, excited anticipation of Your coming.

Chapter 9

HOPE AS A WEAPON

As we continue our study of hope, I trust that you are beginning to grasp the theme of hope in a deeper biblical sense than you may have before. It is my prayer for you that what I have been sharing in this book will give you a solid scriptural understanding of what hope is, how important it is, and how you may have it.

The world tends to think of hope as a nice, positive feeling that cheers us along life's way and comforts us through the hard times. Although there is nothing wrong with that kind of hope, unless it is based on faith it is merely wishful thinking. Most of us aren't prepared for the possibility that we could actually *lose* hope. As we said earlier, it is not until we begin losing hope (or perhaps have already lost it) that we realize the depths to which we truly need it. We not only need hope so we will feel better. We need hope to survive.

Simply put, losing hope can become a matter of life and death, which is part of the reason the enemy of our soul tries so hard to rob us of it. His ultimate goal is to steal, kill, and destroy. But God's plan for us is to give us a future *and a hope.*

> *"For I know the plans that I have for you,"* *declares the Lord, "plans for welfare and not* *for calamity to give you a future and a hope"* (Jeremiah 29:11).

This is why the Bible teaches us that genuine hope is a spiritual weapon—a very important one! Have you ever considered hope in that light? This theme will be the topic of our discussion, not only in this chapter, but also the next.

Provision for Protection

To begin this part of our discussion, we need to understand that as Christians, we are involved in a tremendous spiritual conflict spanning heaven and earth. Our involvement in this spiritual conflict is not optional. We have no choice in the matter. It is mandatory. When we become Christians, as followers of the Lord Jesus Christ, we are automatically involved in this conflict with the powers of Satan and of darkness. Nowhere does this battle rage more powerfully than in our own minds.

Paul speaks about this in Ephesians 6:10–12:

> *Finally, be strong in the Lord and in the strength of His might. Put on the full armor of God, so that you will be able to stand firm against the schemes of the devil.* [Notice we are in direct conflict with the devil.] *For our struggle is not against flesh and blood* [Another translation says it is not against "persons with bodies." We are struggling against unseen spiritual forces.], *but against the rulers, against the powers, against the world forces of this darkness, against the spiritual forces of wickedness in the heavenly places.*

Notice that our conflict is not just happening on the earthly plane; it is also on the heavenly plane. As I said earlier, this conflict spans heaven and earth. Paul then gives us the practical application of these verses in Ephesians 6:13:

> *Therefore, take up the full armor of God, so that you will be able to resist in the evil day, and having done everything, to stand firm.*

I want to point out to you that we are not born with the armor in place, even when we are born again. We are born with the *potential* for putting on the armor of God. But we must take it up ourselves. It does not simply drop down on us.

BATTLE READY

In the verses quoted above, we also see that Paul does not say the evil day *may* come. He says you and I are going to experience it. Every one of us will encounter the evil day at some point. Be ready for it. Be fully armed. Notice his emphasis on the *full* armor.

As you read the verses that follow, keep in mind that Paul is identifying specific pieces of armor we will need to face the evil day.

Stand firm therefore, having girded your loins with truth, and having put on the breastplate of righteousness, and having shod your feet with the preparation of the gospel of peace; in addition to all, taking up the shield of faith with which you will be able to extinguish all the flaming arrows of the evil one. And take the helmet of salvation, and the sword of the Spirit, which is the word of God (Ephesians 6:14–17).

We see that there are six pieces of armor, which I will list here:

1. The girdle or belt of truth

2. The breastplate of righteousness

3. The shoes of the preparation of the gospel of peace

4. The shield of faith

5. The helmet of salvation

6. The sword of the Spirit, the Word of God

Actually, the complete list is sevenfold. There are six items of equipment, plus a seventh weapon. What is that weapon? It is the one which Charles Wesley, in one of his hymns, calls "the weapon of all prayer"—praying always with all prayer and supplication in the Spirit. The next verse, verse 18, tells us more about this additional weapon.

> *With all prayer and petition pray at all times in the Spirit, and with this in view, be on the alert with all perseverance and petition for all the saints* (Ephesians 6:18).

How do we effectively activate the weapons? Through prayer.

As I studied this list I came to realize that if a believer puts on each piece of equipment, he is completely protected from the crown of his head to the soles of his feet—upon one condition. What is that condition? That he doesn't turn his back. Why? Because there is no protection for the back.

STAYING IN THE BATTLE

If you turn your back, if you give up, if you say, "It's no good, I can't do it anymore, I'm giving up," then you are turning a defenseless back to the devil. In your despair you may not realize it, but that is what you are doing.

And believe me, the devil will pour in his fiery darts and wound you in the back. We have to stay facing the enemy.

What can cause a Christian to give up and turn his defenseless back to the enemy? Throughout the years of my ministry, I have consistently seen one circumstance that can cause even the most dedicated, faithful Christian to give up. It is not tragedy, loss, or a personal setback. It is hopelessness.

As I have said many times already in this book, the reason I share such a deep concern for Christians who are struggling with hopelessness is my own experience. My concern for you stems from a time in my own life, many years ago, when I was in a desperate battle with depression. Even though I was a mature Christian, in full-time ministry, I was losing all hope.

I found out for myself about the wounds that can come from offering a defenseless back to the enemy because of hopelessness. In the next chapter, I will share with you how the Holy Spirit, through the Word of God, not only led me to victory, but taught me how to maintain that victory throughout the rest of my life. It is my sincere prayer that my story will encourage you. I believe that if you are in a difficult battle with hopelessness, the Holy Spirit can do for you what He did for me.

Chapter 10

THE HELMET OF HOPE

IN THIS CHAPTER, LET'S FOCUS OUR ATTENTION ON THE fifth piece of our armor—the helmet of salvation, and its unmistakable connection to what Scripture calls in First Thessalonians 5:8, the helmet of hope of our salvation.

Each one of the seven pieces of armor that Paul lists in the sixth chapter of Ephesians is of vital importance for every believer. But let's focus now on the fifth item—the helmet of salvation. I will tell you in this chapter how it has become an essential part of my own personal victory over depression and hopelessness.

My story begins in the mid-1950s, when I was pastoring a congregation in London, England. During that time, God was in many ways blessing my ministry. We regularly saw people saved, healed, and baptized in the Holy Spirit. Inwardly, however, I was battling a tremendous, ongoing struggle with depression. Those around me never had any idea what was going on inside of me. But almost day and night during this period of my life, I was surrounded by an awful sense of depression. It took the form of a dark, heavy cloud that would descend over me—pressing me down, closing in on me, and shutting me off from normal communication with other people—even my own family.

Ironically, the more successful I became in my ministry, the worse the oppression grew. I battled against it in every way that I could. I prayed. I fasted. I reckoned myself dead. I made resolutions. I got up early. I stayed up late. I did everything within my power that I knew to do. But nothing seemed to do any good. In fact, the more I prayed and fasted, the worse it got.

THE BREAKTHROUGH

Then one day, when I reached the end of all my efforts, God gave me a wonderful revelation. I read these words from Isaiah 61:3, *"The garment of praise for the spirit of heaviness"* (NKJV).

Suddenly, as I read those words—*the spirit of heaviness*—the Holy Spirit indicated to me, "That's your problem. It's not you. It's not a mental or a psychological condition. It is a spirit—it is a person that hates you, that dogs you, that is unseen. It is a person without a body that has followed you even from boyhood. That person knows your weakness, so as to know exactly when and how to attack you most effectively. You are fighting a person, an unseen demonic person. It is the spirit of heaviness."

In modern English we would call it the *spirit of depression*. This was not psychological. I was not dealing merely with some entrenched pattern of negative thinking. There was a person—an evil spirit set against me by Satan himself—tracking me and plotting my downfall.

Then I saw why the pressure got worse the more I wanted to serve the Lord. The assignment of this evil spirit was to hinder me in my service for God. When I was somewhat slack and indifferent in my ministry, the pressure was lifted. But the more dedicated and earnest I became, the worse the pressure became.

SET FREE

At last, I had come to realize the identity of my enemy. With that realization, I knew I was 80 percent of the way to victory. But the Lord knew that I only needed one other scripture to bring me the solution to my problem. He led me to Joel 2:32, which says this:

> *It shall come to pass, that whosoever shall call on the name of the Lord shall be delivered* (KJV).

I saw that this promise was just as all-inclusive as John 3:16:

> *Whosoever believeth in him should not perish, but have everlasting life* (KJV).

I knew that these verses were a promise to me of deliverance, and I said, "That's for me!" I did not understand the deliverance ministry in any sense in which we do now. But driven by my own desperate need, and acting on those promises in faith, I put the two Scriptures together—Isaiah 61:3 and Joel 2:32. Then I prayed *specifically* to God, and I want to emphasize the importance of praying specifically. I named the spirit, "the spirit of heaviness," and

I claimed God's own promise, "Whoever shall call on the name of the Lord shall be delivered."

This was my prayer: "God, in the name of the Lord Jesus Christ, according to Your Word, I'm asking You to deliver me from this spirit of heaviness." When I prayed that specific, scriptural prayer, I was delivered! The pressure was lifted! I give God all the thanks and praise for this wonderful, wonderful deliverance.

Chapter 11

WEARING THE HELMET

AS JOYFUL AS I WAS AT THE TIME OF THE DELIVERANCE I described in the previous chapter, I quickly learned that it is one thing to be delivered—it is another challenge altogether to *stay* delivered. God began to show me that He had done His part of the job. Now I had to do my part. I had to learn how to protect my own mind against thoughts of pessimism, morbidity, and depression.

As I considered how to protect my mind, I remembered these words in Ephesians 6, "the helmet of salvation."

Immediately I said to myself, "That's what I must have—the helmet of salvation."

So I came to realize my need for this helmet of salvation to protect my mind. But then I wondered, "What *is* the helmet of salvation? I know I'm saved—doesn't that mean I have the helmet of salvation already? If I have it already, why do I need to take another step?"

The answer to my questions came when I realized that the people to whom Paul wrote in Ephesians were like me—they were saved and had received the Holy Spirit. Yet Paul still told them to put on the helmet of salvation. Therefore, the fact that a person is saved does not mean that he or she is wearing the armor. Saved people must still put on the armor of God. So I began to explore more fully what exactly the helmet of salvation is.

Fortunately, in the margin of my Bible there was a reference for the verse about the helmet in Ephesians. It directed me to First Thessalonians 5:8:

> *But since we are of the day, let us be sober, having put on the breastplate of faith and love, and as a helmet, the hope of salvation.*

This verse refers to two of the pieces of armor that are mentioned in Ephesians 6. The first is the breastplate. It is very obvious that the breastplate of faith and love protects the heart. (As I said earlier, faith is in the heart.)

Then the verse continues: *"And as a helmet, the hope of salvation."* When I read those words, I felt as if currents of divine electricity were going right through me! I said to myself, "That's the helmet—it's hope!"

Reclaiming My Mind

Faith is in the heart and protects the heart. But hope is in the mind and protects the mind. Immediately I saw that one of my biggest problem areas in my life was in the realm of my mind. All through my life, the devil had been continually reaching in and defeating me through my mind. His attack on my mind came in two ways.

The first way was through my education. I happened to have had the privilege of a very elaborate, prolonged, and scholarly education, especially in the area of analytical thinking. I discovered that the more highly refined and cultivated a person's mind is, the more vulnerable that person can be to Satan. Why? In my case, I realized that the more I trusted in and relied upon my own mind, the more Satan could use it against me. I was going to have to learn how to reclaim control of my mind.

Second, I realized that all through my life I had been a habitual pessimist. Not only that, the whole of my family background was one of pessimism. I respect my parents and I am grateful for their memory, but they were steeped in anxiety and pessimism. I would have to say that in my family if you were not worrying about something, you ought to be worrying about the fact you were not worrying! As a result, I was totally imbued with this spirit of worrying and pessimism.

God then began to reveal to me that this pessimism was actually a denial of my faith. If I truly believed the gospel, I could not be a pessimist. In earlier chapters, we considered several scriptures which teach this very clearly, especially Romans 8:28:

> *And we know that God causes all things to work together for good to those who love God, to those who are called according to His purpose.*

God said in effect, "I've delivered you from a spirit of depression. Now, it is up to you to put on the helmet of salvation, which is the helmet of hope." As a result, I began a process of retraining my mind. I had to cultivate a totally different outlook, different reactions, different mental patterns. Every time a negative or pessimistic thought would come to my mind I would refuse to yield to it. I also quoted and memorized helpful Scriptures that became a scriptural foundation for not being a pessimist, but for being an optimist!

Changes did not happen overnight, or even in a period of months. Change happened over a period of years. However, I can testify that I became a totally different person from what I was before this experience. I am now a scriptural, Bible-believing optimist. In addition, thanks to what God showed me in Scripture, I keep my helmet on day and night. I *never* take that helmet off—the helmet of optimistic hope. It is a helmet that ensures faith in God and hope in Him, and protects my mind against all the dark forces of pessimism and depression.

BREAKING THE CHAINS

In the years since my deliverance, I have helped many people who have suffered from prolonged, serious depression. I have come to the conclusion that in almost every case, it is connected with involvement in the occult.

This was true in my own situation. Before I became a believer, my involvement in the occult had been quite extensive, particularly in the field of yoga. It was not until many years later that I saw the connection between my involvement with yoga and the spirit of depression.

My ministry in the area of deliverance has spanned many decades now. I can tell you clearly that whenever I deal with a person who has prolonged, serious bouts of depression, it is usually a signal to me that somewhere along the line, they have trespassed into Satan's territory in the realm of the occult. If you are depressed and you suspect that occult involvement is part of the issue, it is of the utmost importance that you deal with that issue. You must first take back the ground that has been given to the enemy. In fact, for me to tell you to cultivate new thought patterns would be like a drill sergeant giving orders to a group of soldiers who are fettered. They can hear the orders, but their feet can't move to carry the orders out.

Deliverance is an essential part of God's provision. If your depression or hopelessness is a demonic problem, then step number one is deliverance from the demon. Once that is dealt with, step number two is to begin a "retraining program"—to bring your thoughts into captivity to the obedience of Christ.[1]

NOTE

1. If you believe your hopelessness or depression
    is possibly the result of demonic oppression,
    additional teaching on this topic is available in
    The Basics of Deliverance CD set and study guide
    by Derek Prince. Please contact either Destiny
    Image Publications at destinyimage.com or Derek
    Prince Ministries at derekprince.org to obtain
    these materials.

Chapter 12

HOPE AS AN ANCHOR

IN OUR PREVIOUS TWO CHAPTERS, I SHARED MY personal story of how the Lord brought me through a difficult battle with hopelessness into lasting victory. Through the Scriptures, He led me to understand that hope is absolutely essential, a vital piece of spiritual armor. Had I never gone through that desperate crisis, I might never have gained the proper understanding of the place of hope in the life of the believer and its importance for the protection of our minds. This understanding has set me free and changed my life.

My testimony of wearing the helmet of hope—every day and night—can be yours as well. It is my prayer that what I have shared will help you to always put on the helmet of hope.

In this closing chapter, I want to present you with another beautiful picture of hope as an anchor of the soul. This is not only a beautiful aspect of hope. As we shall see, it is another practical tool for allowing hope to govern our lives!

PICTURES FROM HEBREWS

To begin, we are going to explore a lengthy passage from Hebrews 6:11–20, which actually gives us two pictures of hope. The first is as the horns of an altar. The second is as an anchor of the soul. Let's begin at verse 11:

> *And we desire that each one of you show the same diligence so as to realize the full assurance of hope until the end.*

Please notice that the emphasis is on maintaining hope until the end. This thought parallels the perseverance of hope which we have discussed in an earlier chapter.

So that you will not be sluggish [or lazy], but imitators of those who through faith and patience inherit the promises (Hebrews 6:12).

Faith and Patience

The writer of Hebrews then gives us Abraham as the example of an individual who inherited the promises through faith and patience:

For when God made the promise to Abraham, since He could swear by no one greater, He swore by Himself, saying, "I will surely bless you and I will surely multiply you." And so, having patiently waited, he [Abraham] obtained the promise (Hebrews 6:13–14).

Immediately, the writer goes on to explain why God swore to Abraham with an oath:

For men swear by one greater than themselves, and with them an oath given as confirmation is an end of every dispute. In the same way God, desiring even more to show to the heirs of the promise the unchangeableness of His purpose, interposed with an oath, so that by two

unchangeable things in which it is impossible for
God to lie, we who have taken refuge would have
strong encouragement to take hold of the hope set
before us (Hebrews 6:16–18).

We need to emphasize some important truths before
we continue. First, hope must be maintained until the
end; it is associated with diligence, faith, perseverance,
and patience. In fact, hope is the key to perseverance
and patience.

Notice also that God desires that our confidence should
be based upon two unchangeable pillars. The first is His
Word; the second is His oath. God's spoken word really is
sufficient. However, in certain situations, to convince us
that He absolutely means what He says and will *never* go
back on His word, He confirms the word He has given us
by His oath.

The writer of Hebrews then makes a practical application to hope:

That by two immutable things, in which it is
impossible for God to lie, we might have strong
consolation, who have fled for refuge to lay hold
of the hope set before us (Hebrews 6:18 NKJV).

HOPE AS A REFUGE

There is the first picture of hope we talked about earlier—it is a refuge. In order to fully appreciate what the writer is saying, we need to understand the Old Testament custom from which this picture is taken.

In Old Testament times, when a man was being pursued by an enemy who was attempting to take his life, there was one place where he was guaranteed security. If he could run to the altar of God and catch hold of the horns of the altar (on the altar there were four horns, one at each corner) no one would dare to pull that man away from the horns of the altar. (See First Kings 1:50–53.)

Here is what the writer of Hebrews is saying: Hope is like taking hold of the horns of the altar. When the enemy is pursuing you, when he is breathing down your neck to the point that there seems to be no way of escape, your place of refuge is the horns of the altar. Find them. Cling to them.

What are the horns of the altar? The horns of the altar represent the hope God has given us in these two immutable gifts: first, *His word*; second, *His oath*. If, as you are reading this, you are under intense pressure, wondering where to turn, I recommend you turn to the altar. The altar is the place of sacrifice that represents the death of Jesus Christ on our behalf. Lay hold of the horns of hope there at that altar. When you do, you will be secure. Because the enemy, the accuser, and the avenger will not be able to follow you there.

HOPE AS AN ANCHOR

The second picture of hope in this passage is in verses 19 and 20. To me, this analogy is the most beautiful of all the pictures of hope. Because of my own struggles and need for hope, it is the principle that means so much to me personally. This is what the writer of Hebrews says:

> *This hope we have as an anchor of the soul, a hope both sure and steadfast and one which enters within the veil* [the second veil into the Holy of Holies], *where Jesus has entered as a forerunner for us, having become a high priest forever according to the order of Melchizedek* (Hebrews 6:19–20).

In this passage, hope is pictured as an anchor of the soul. It is described as sure and steadfast. In addition, this anchor enters in within the veil. It passes out of time into eternity. It is fastened into the Rock of Ages, attached to the very presence of Almighty God.

I found this beautiful passage when I was struggling with the pessimism that dogged my steps. My background as a philosopher prompted me to approach this passage analytically and logically. As I meditated on these words, I carried on a dialogue within myself.

I said, "Hope is an anchor."

Then I asked, "What needs an anchor?"

I answered my own question: "A boat needs an anchor."

"Why does a boat need an anchor?"

"Because a boat is made to float on water, which is a totally unstable element."

My thought process was absolutely correct. There is nothing in water that you can fasten on to that will keep you from being tossed about by the waves. Therefore, in order to be held secure, the boat must pass its anchor through the unstable water into some completely secure object that will hold it steady. The best example is a rock.

When I thought about my own life, I had to admit: "Sometimes I feel I'm like that little boat tossed to and fro on the waves."

Without question, I recognized that all human beings live in a world which is temporal, impermanent, and insecure. There is nothing for us to fasten on to in this world which will guarantee us security. Therefore, for true stability, we must have an anchor which passes out of time into eternity. It must pass out of the temporal, the material, the unstable, and the changeable into something that is permanent, unchangeable, totally stable, and secure.

OUR FORERUNNER

As I pondered this undeniable truth, I saw so clearly and beautifully that the anchor I have is my hope in Jesus. It is not restricted to time. It does not depend upon material possessions. Its security is not found in the frailty of human beings and human institutions. It is based on two unchangeable provisions in which it is impossible for God to lie—His word and His oath.

You and I can pass our anchor right out of time into the immediate presence of God. We can pass beyond that second veil into that holy place where Jesus has already entered as my personal representative—my forerunner and my high priest. Trusting in Jesus, I am not limited to this world or to the constraints of time. All the treasures of this world upon which people depend for security are transient—they are going to pass away. But my anchor of eternal hope reaches out beyond this world into the immediate presence of God.

It is so profound to realize what the writer of Hebrews says:

> *Where Jesus has entered as a forerunner for us, having become a high priest forever according to the order of Melchizedek* (Hebrews 6:20).

The function of our High Priest is to represent before God those who trust in Him. The writer of Hebrews is also referring to Jesus as our High Priest when he says:

> *He is able also to save forever those who draw near to God through Him, since He always lives to make intercession for them* (Hebrews 7:25).

Our High Priest, who is in the immediate presence of God, is always making intercession for us. He never sleeps. He is never going to die because He lives forever. He is our personal representative before Almighty God. The writer of Hebrews also tells us that *"Jesus Christ the same yesterday and today and forever"* (Hebrews 13:8). He is the eternal rock in which our hope is anchored.

OUR ETERNAL ROCK

As we conclude this chapter and bring this book to a close, let's take a moment to reflect on the profound truth of our hope being anchored to the eternal rock, Jesus Christ.

Everything around us may, at times, seem unstable and shaky—a swirl of change and uncertainty. It can be enough to cause us to slip into fear, dismay, and hopelessness. But then comes the picture of us throwing out our anchor by faith, calling out the name of Jesus as we do. At His name, our anchor passes through unstable time into eternity—sinking deep into the Rock of Ages, holding strong and firm in Jesus.

Can we end with a simple prayer of thanks?

> *Thank You, Jesus, that the hope I have is firmly anchored in You. By Your word and Your oath, I come to You as my refuge and the anchor of my soul. Thank You, Lord, that*

instead of being tossed to and fro by every
wave that hits, I am stable and secure in You.
I fully place my life and my trust in You. You
alone are my hope in a hopeless world. Amen.

Now that you have told the Lord that He is your hope, please add to that prayer this powerful proclamation:

PROCLAMATION FOR UNSHAKABLE HOPE

My God turns my darkness into light[1]

The Lord is my inheritance;
therefore, I will hope in Him![2]

I will call upon the Lord and He will be with me

In difficult times, He will deliver
me. He is my salvation.[3]

God sees my trouble and considers my grief.[4]

He is my Helper.[5]

I destroy every obstacle that keeps
me from knowing God.

I take all negative thoughts captive

And teach them to obey Christ.[6]

The God of hope fills me with all joy and peace,

So that I may overflow with hope by
the power of the Holy Spirit.[7]

When doubts fill my mind,

His comfort gives me new hope and cheer.[8]

I'm anxious about nothing,
but in every situation

I tell the Lord, with thanksgiving, my needs.

The peace of God, which surpasses
all my own thinking,

Will guard my heart and my
mind in Christ Jesus.

Whatever is true, noble and right, pure, lovely

And excellent, I think about such things.[9]

God will uphold me with His
righteous right hand.[10]

God will restore, support, and strengthen me,

And He will place me on a firm foundation.[11]

The Lord has plans to prosper
me, not to harm me.

He has plans to give me hope and a future.[12]

1. Psalm 18:28 NIV
2. Lamentations 3:24 NLT
3. Psalm 91:15-16 NIV
4. Psalm 10:14 NIV
5. Psalm 118:7 NIV
6. 2 Corinthians 10:5 NLT
7. Romans 15:13 NIV
8. Psalm 94:19 NLT
9. Philippians 4:6-8 NIV
10. Isaiah 41:10 NIV
11. 1 Peter 5:10 NLT
12. Jeremiah 29:11 NIV

About Derek Prince

Derek Prince (1915–2003) founded Derek Prince Ministries International and authored more than eighty books during his lifetime. He studied at Eton College, Cambridge University, and at the Hebrew University in Jerusalem. His daily radio broadcast, Derek Prince Legacy Radio, still reaches listeners around the world.